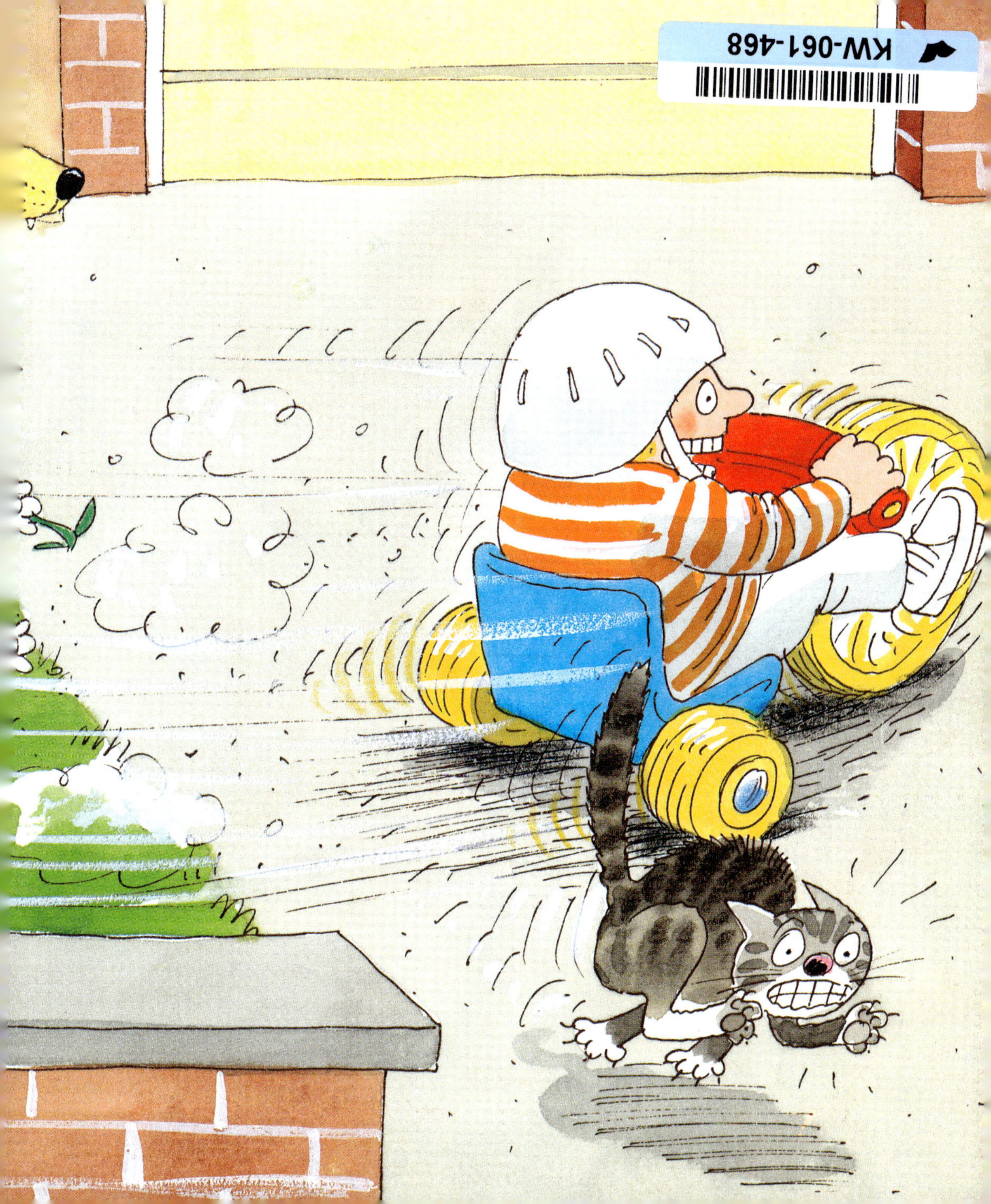

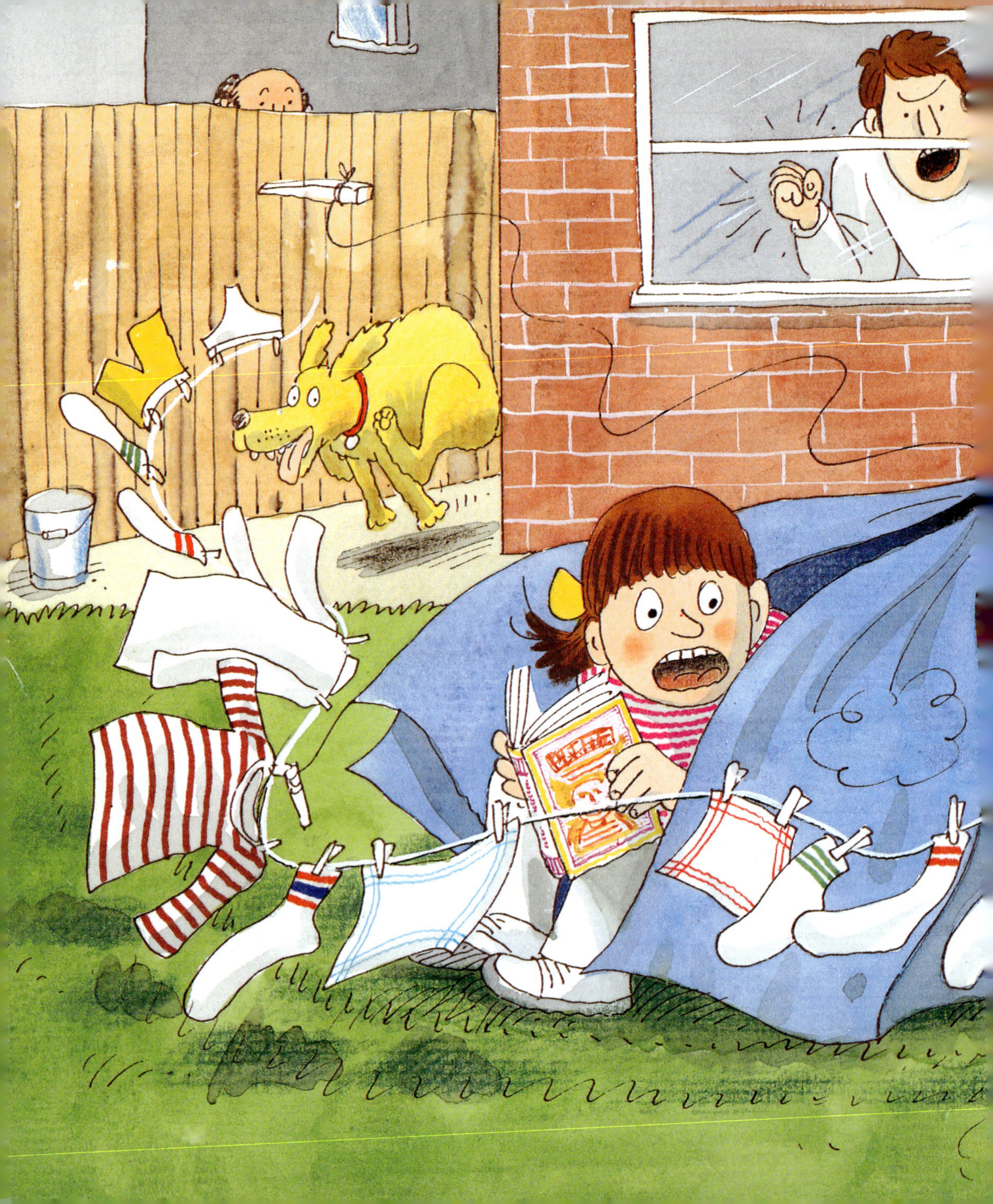

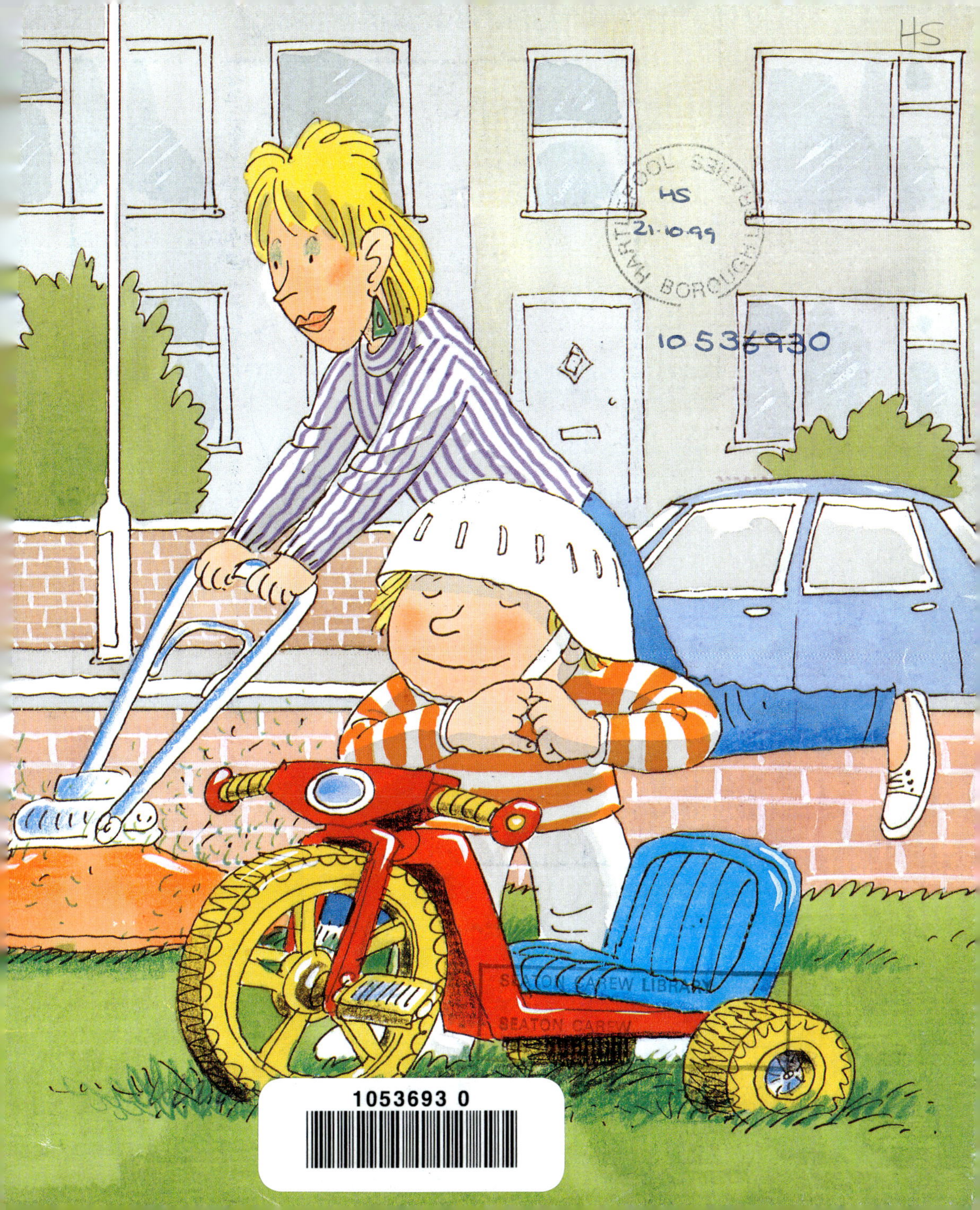

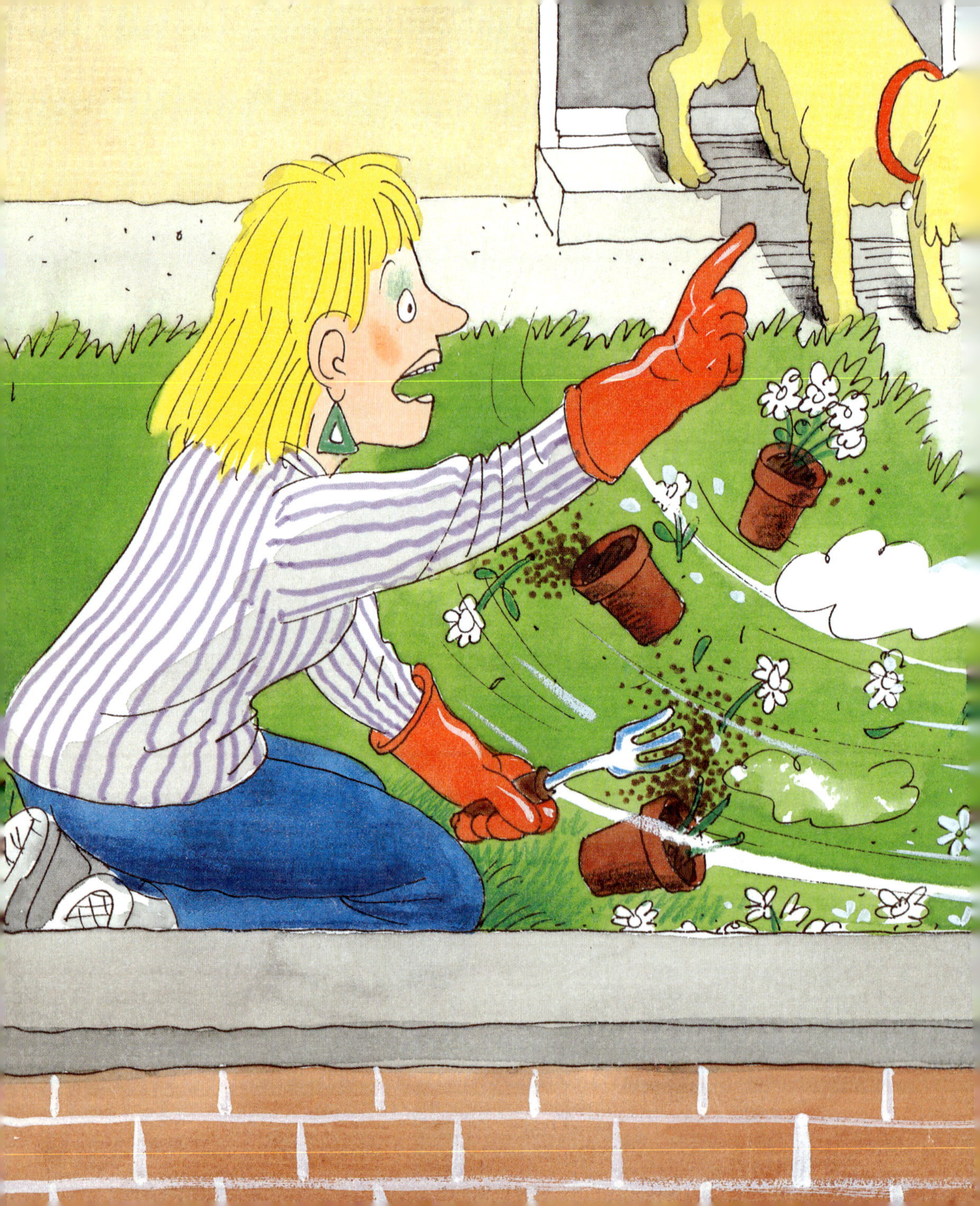

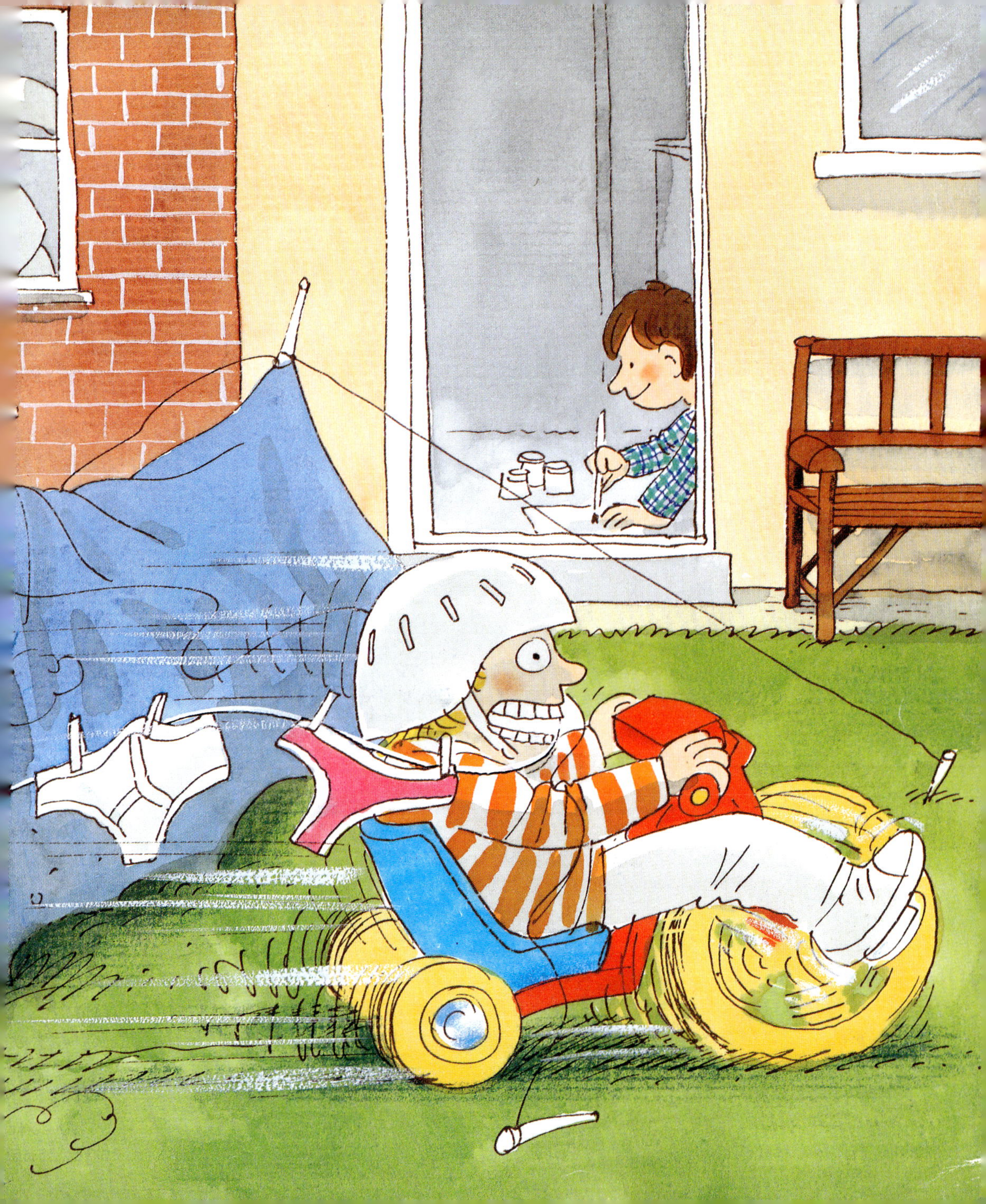

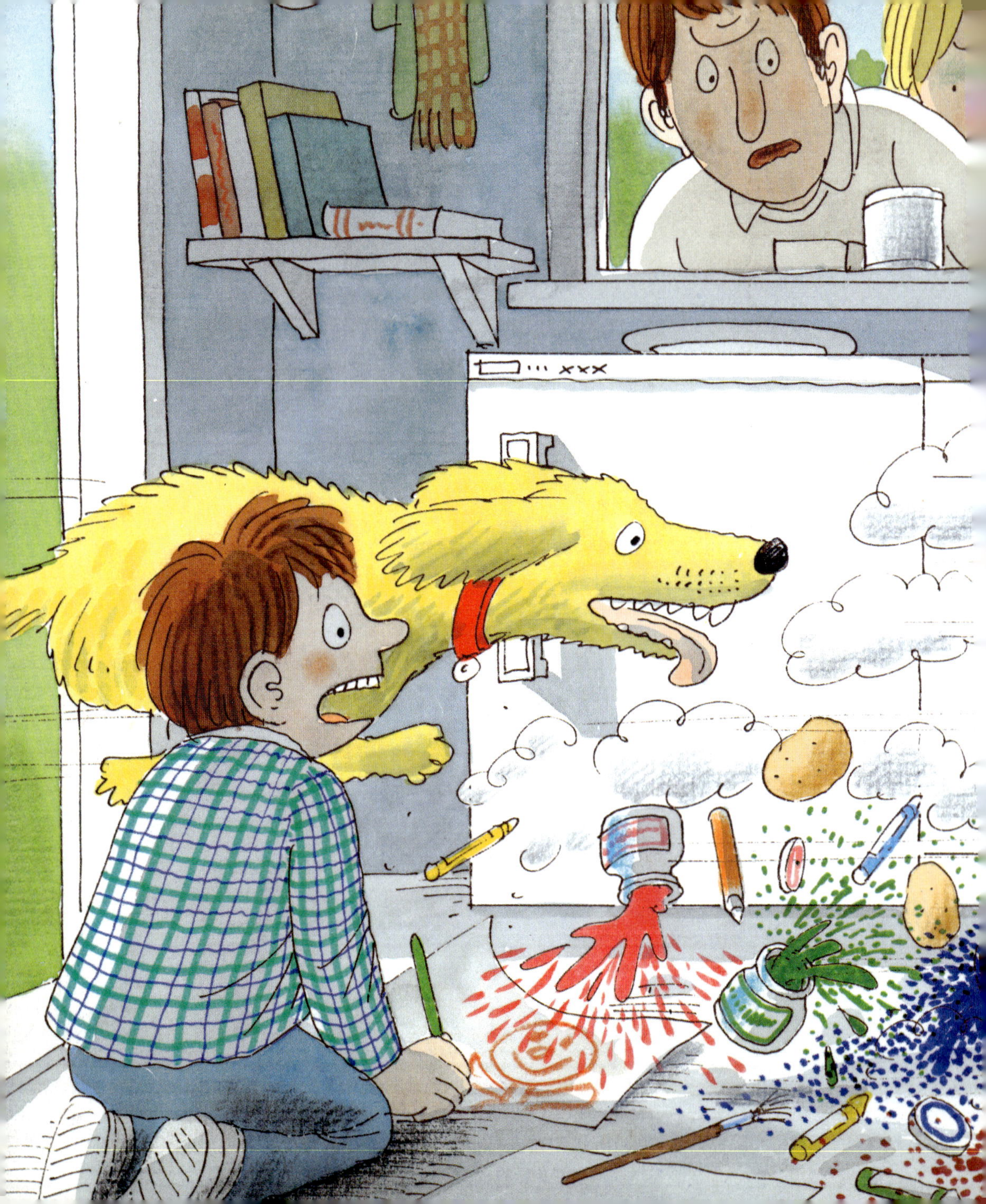

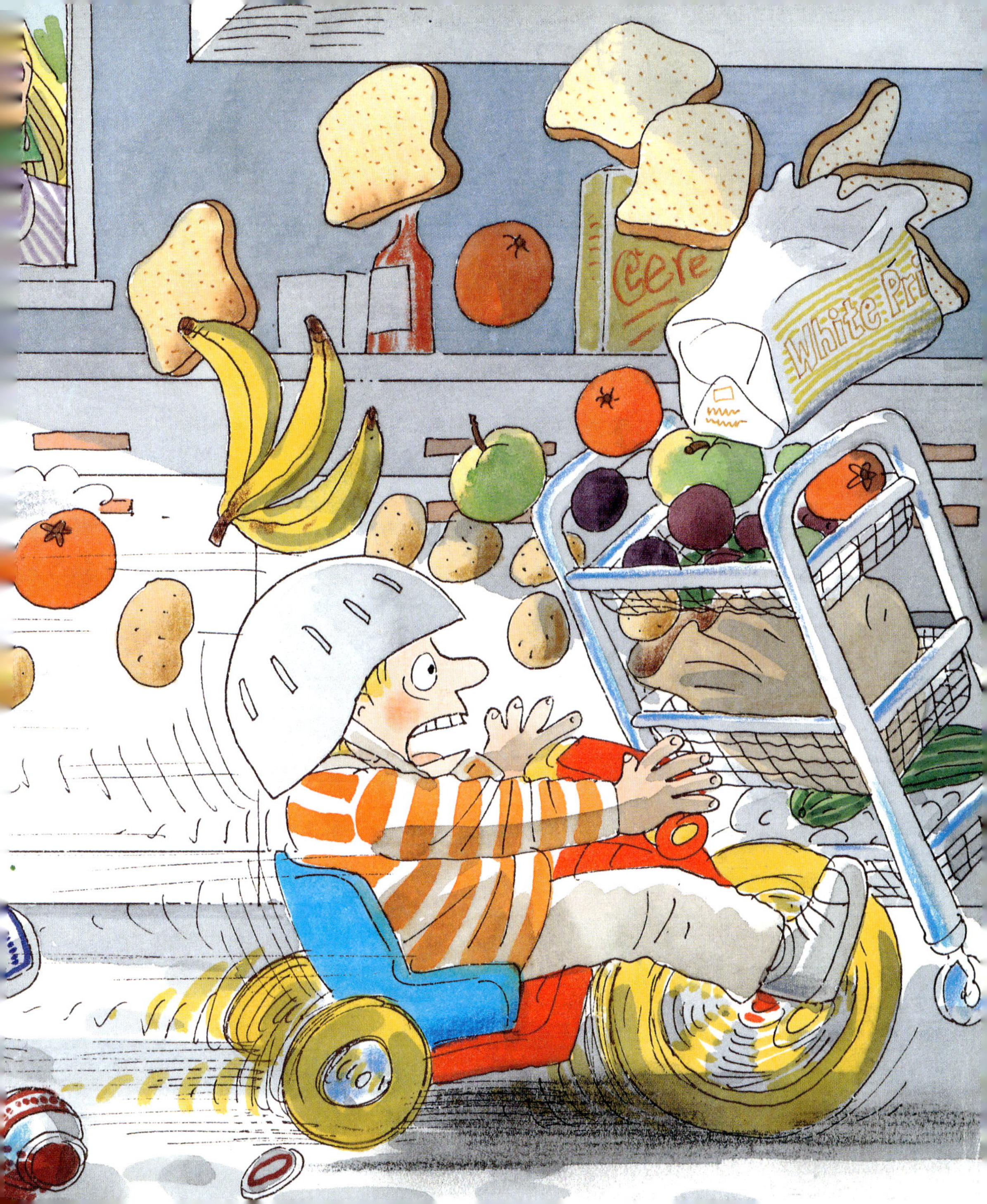
Cere
White Pri

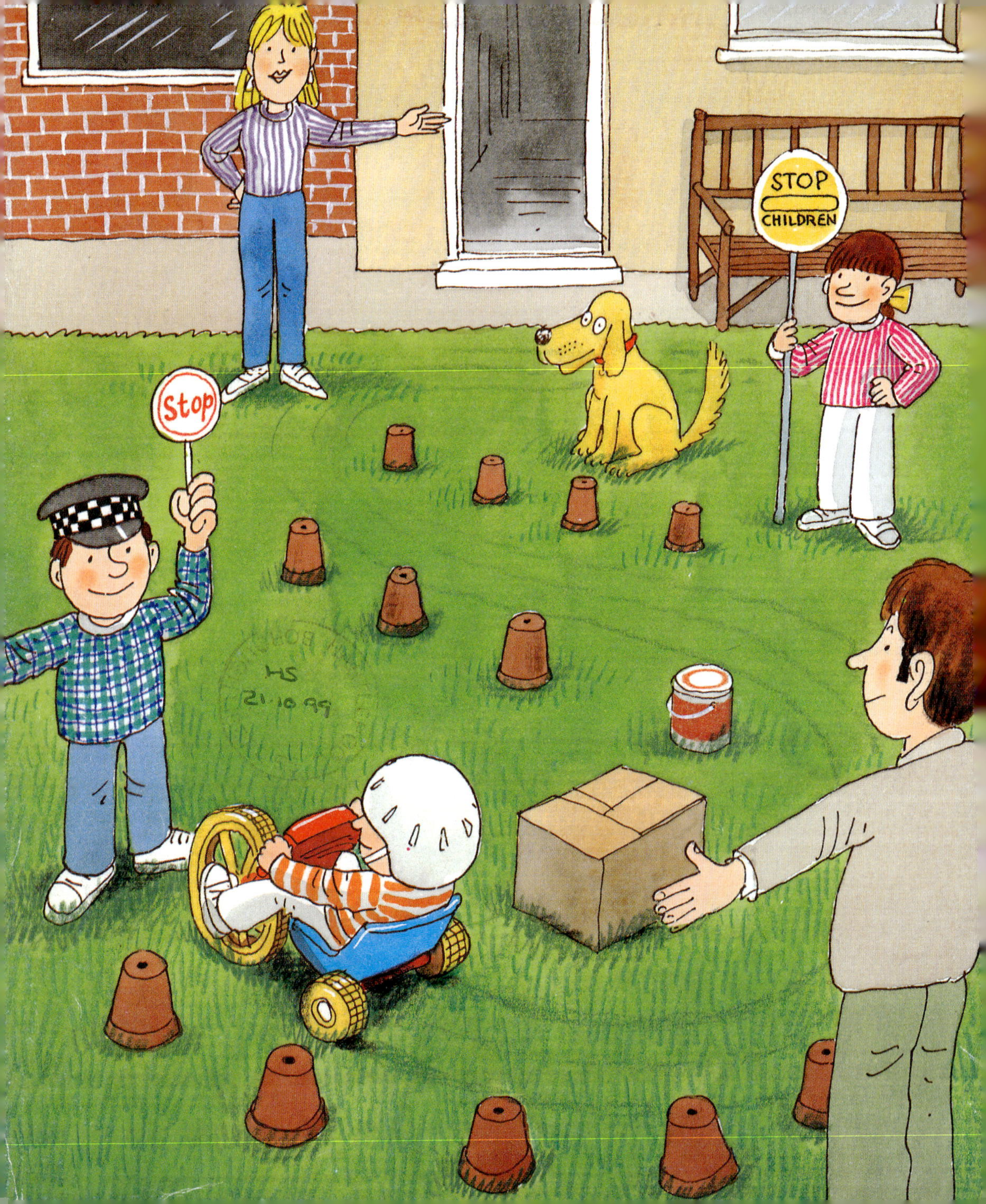
Stop
STOP
CHILDREN